"You are not far from the Kingdom of God."

MARK 12. 34
JESUS TO THE JEWISH SCRIBE:

"You are not far from the Kingdom of God."

One hundred sayings of Jesus, plus their Hebrew sources, that reveal the Anti-Christianity of Anti-Semitism

by Eugene M. Schwartz

SECOND CREATION PRESS, INC.

My thanks to Jillen Lowe, Bill Magee, Sam Magee and Roberta Waddell for their infinite patience in helping me with this meticulous task. And to Mark Aaron, Bill Anastasi, Dean James Morton, Elaine Pagels, and Jerry Shestack for their comments and corrections on the early drafts.

Second Creation Press, Inc.
210 East 86th Street – Suite 501
New York, New York 10028

Graphic Design by: Kingsley Parker, Ed Noriega and Tony Cinturati

Library of Congress Cataloging-in-Publication Data

Schwartz, Eugene M.
    You are not far from the kingdom of God : a plea for the re-establishment of Jewish-Christian brotherhood / by Eugene M. Schwartz

    p. ca.
    Includes bibliographical references.
    ISBN 0-9633139-0-8 : $30.00 (approx.)
    1. Jesus Christ—Teachings. 2. Bible. N.T.—Relation to the Old Testament. 3. Bible. O.T.—Quotations in the New Testament.

I. Title.
BS2415. A28383 1992
220.6'5—dc20   92-16764

TABLE OF CONTENTS

DEDICATION

To the millions of Christians and Jews
who have loved each other.

Who, as Christians,
share in the kingdom,
and the power, and the glory.
As Jesus states in Matthew 6.13.

And who, as Jews,
share in the power,
and the glory, and the kingdom.
As David states in 1 Chronicles 29.10-11.

INTRODUCTION

This is a book for every man and woman — Christian or Jew — who loves God and despises hate. . . especially the hate called Anti-Semitism.

This book has been designed to display 100 sayings of Jesus, side by side with their sources in the Hebrew scriptures, in order to reveal — parallel saying by parallel saying — the inherent Anti-Christianity of Anti-Semitism.

More specifically, it attempts to show this: that much of the love in Jesus's words comes from the love in the words of the Judaism that preceded him, of which he was a fervent follower.

To establish the authority and depth of his message, he carefully searched the Hebrew scriptures. He then — like the Jewish sages before him — chose from the great monuments of faith and love that had been formulated in the thousand years before he rose to speak.

He was a master of paraphrase and condensation. And from the truths that came before him, he rephrased and wove many together — this too had been done time after time before him — to create the new meanings which he hoped to add to that heritage.

For example, in the Beatitudes and elsewhere, he introduced a strong repetitive structure to tie several older, separate precepts together.

In the Lord's Prayer, he called upon, by reference, the pivotal moments of Jewish history in ten simple phrases.

In the Sermon on the Mount, as a whole, he gave us perhaps the greatest summary of Jewish ethics and love ever assembled -- which became simultaneously the beginnings of Christian ethics and love.

And, throughout, he replaced the older symbols of God's glory — "delivered my soul from death", "the holy place", etc.— with his own symbols — "resurrection", "The Kingdom of God", etc.

However, in the two thousand years that followed his death, many of these parallels between the Hebrew Scriptures and the New Testament have been overlooked. Since I have not found them placed side by side in the literature, this book does that.

Its structure is simple. First, what seems to be the Jewish sources are presented on the left page — and then, on the right page, what seems to be Jesus' adaptation of them.

If more than one source was used, I have joined them to resemble as closely as possible the phrasing of Jesus' statement. In doing this, I have followed the methods used continually, not only by Jesus, but by the Jewish writers who preceded him. (See notes in Appendix on interweaving.)

Wherever this was done, I have used three dots (. . .) to indicate the joining.

I have also left out words in the original sources, where necessary, to shorten them and emphasize that parallelism. But I have not changed the order of their words. And at the book's end, the full text of the original sources is given.

Finally, I have followed Second Isaiah and John, for example, in making pronouns, intransitive verbs and prepositions cohere in each rewoven verse.

Most of these parallelisms have been recognized by Christianity for centuries. Many more than I have used here, for example, are given in the concordance and the center columns of the World Book edition of the King James Bible. (See note in Appendix on the number of World Book listings.)

In fact, there seems now to be little new in this book. For example, on pages 673 and 904 of The New American Bible are listed the two Hebraic sources of Matthew 5.39 — **"Do not resist evil. If someone smite you on the left cheek, give him the right cheek as well."** These sources are listed there as Proverb 20.22 — **"Do not say, 'I will repay evil,'"** — and Lamentations 3.30 — **He gives his cheek to him that smites it."**

Finally, I have not dealt in any way with the question of the relation of Jesus' words to Matthew, Mark, Luke, or John. I have simply taken the words as they are now presented in the King James and other Christian Bibles.

The perspective of this book is simple. It is that of Jesus as a great Jewish rabbi and teacher. He spoke to his people, and then to all people, to help lead them closer to their one God.

It is the same Father for both Jew and Christian. We are brother and sister religions. This book is a reminder that we come from that same Father, and are blessed by that Father when we achieve the same end. . . love.

The words — in both great religions — speak for themselves.

THE GREAT COMMANDMENTS

LEVITICUS 19.18

**"You shall love your neighbor
as yourself."**

"You shall love your neighbor
as yourself."

"Hear, O Israel;
   the Lord our God
is one Lord."

"Hear, O Israel;
 the Lord our God
is one."

DEUTERONOMY 6.5

"You shall love the Lord your God
    with all your heart,
and with all your soul,
    and with all your might."

"You shall love the Lord your God
    with all your heart,
and with all your soul,
    and with all your mind,
and with all your strength."

THE BOND BETWEEN
JEW AND CHRISTIAN

The Jewish scribe to Jesus:

"You are right, Teacher;
　　you have truly said that He is one,
and there is no other but He;
　　and to love Him with all your heart,
and with all your strength,
　　and with all your understanding,
and to love one's neighbor as oneself,
　　is much more than all
the whole burnt offerings and sacrifices."

Jesus to the Jewish scribe:

**"You are not far
from the kingdom of God."**

THE SERMON ON THE MOUNT

Isaiah 52.7

"How beautiful upon the mountains
    are the feet of him who
    brings good tidings,
who publishes peace, who brings
    good tidings of good,
    who publishes salvation,
who says to Zion, your God reigns!"

THE BEATITUDES

PSALM 32.2 . . . ISAIAH 66.2. . . 57.15

"Blessed is he. . .
    that is poor of spirit. . .
I dwell in
    the high and holy place with him."

"Blessed are
    the poor in spirit,
for theirs is
    the kingdom of heaven."

Isaiah 61.1-2

"The spirit of the Lord God
is upon me,
to comfort all who mourn."

MATTHEW 5.4

"Blessed are those who mourn,
    for they
shall be comforted."

PSALM 37.11

**"The meek shall
inherit the earth."**

MATTHEW 5.5

"Blessed are the meek, for they shall inherit the earth."

"Hungry and thirsty,
    their soul fainted in them.
And He led them forth by the right way,
    and filled their hungry soul
with goodness."

"Blessed are they which do
hunger and thirst
after righteousness:
for they shall be filled."

PSALM 18.25

**"With the merciful,
You will show Yourself merciful."**

"Blessed are the merciful,
 for they shall obtain mercy."

PSALM 24.4 . . . JOB 19.26

**"He who has a pure heart . . .
shall see God."**

**"Blessed are the pure in heart,
for they shall see God."**

"The work of the righteous
    shall be peace . . .
It shall be said to them, 'You are
    the sons of God'."

"Blessed are the peacemakers,
   for they shall be called
the sons of God."

"Hearken to me, you who know
　　righteousness,
fear not the reproach of men,
and be not dismayed at their
　　revilings.
My deliverance will be forever."

"Blessed are they who are persecuted
    for righteousness's sake;
for theirs is the kingdom of heaven.
Blessed are you when men shall revile
    you, and persecute you,
and shall say all manner of evil
    against you falsely for my sake."

ISAIAH 66.10 . . . GENESIS 15.1

"Rejoice, and be glad . . .
for the Lord God is
your exceeding great reward."

"Rejoice, and be
exceedingly glad,
for great is your reward
in heaven."

THE LORD'S PRAYER

1 Chronicles 29.10-11

"Our Father, in heaven,"

MATTHEW 6.9

"Our Father which art in heaven,"

LEVITICUS 22.32

"My name will be hallowed."

MATTHEW 6.9

"Hallowed be thy name."

Exodus 19.6

"You shall be to Me
    a kingdom of priests,
and a holy nation."

**"Thy kingdom
come."**

"But will God dwell
    with men on earth?
Behold,
    heaven cannot contain thee."

"Thy will be done
on earth,
as it is
in heaven."

EXODUS 16.12

"In the morning you
　　shall be filled with bread;
and you shall know that I am
　　the Lord your God."

"Give us this day
our daily bread."

"Say to Joseph, 'Forgive the trespass
of thy brethren;
forgive the trespass of the servants
of the God of thy father'.
And Joseph said to them, 'Fear not,
I will nourish you'."

MATTHEW 6.12

"And forgive us our trespasses,
as we forgive those
who trespass against us."

GENESIS 22.1-2

"And it came to pass
    that God did tempt Abraham;
and He said, take now
    your only son, Isaac,
and offer him for a
    burnt offering."

**"And deliver us not
into temptation,"**

JOB 5.17-19

"The Almighty will deliver you
from evil."

**"But deliver us
from evil."**

1 Chronicles 29.10-11

"For ever, thine is the power,
and the glory, and the kingdom."

"For thine is the kingdom, and the power, and the glory, for ever."

LOVE YOUR ENEMIES – 1

Proverb 24.29

"Say not, 'As he did to me,
    so will I do to him;
I will repay the man
    according to his deeds'."

"You have heard that it was said,
 'An eye for an eye
and a tooth for a tooth'.
 But I say to you . . . "

"Do not say,
   'I will repay evil'. . .
Give your cheek
   to him that smites you."

"You have heard that it was said,
    'An eye for an eye
and a tooth for a tooth'.
    But I say to you,
Do not resist evil:
    but whoever shall smite you
on the right cheek,
    turn to him the other also."

Exodus 23.4-5

"If you meet your enemy's ox
    or his ass going astray,
you shall bring it
    back to him.
If you see the ass of
    him that hates you
lying under its burden,
    you shall refrain from
leaving him with it,
    and you shall help him
lift it up."

"You have heard that it was said,
   'An eye for an eye
and a tooth for a tooth'.
   But I say to you,
Do not resist evil:
   but whoever shall smite you
on the right cheek,
   turn to him the other also.
And if a man will sue you at law,
   and take away your coat,
let him have your cloak also.
   And whoever shall compel you
to go a mile,
   go with him an extra mile."

2 Samuel 19.6

Joab, to King David:

"You
    love your enemies."

"Love your enemies,

PSALMS 109.28-29

Let them curse,
but You bless."

"Love your enemies,
 bless them that curse you."

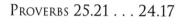
"If your enemy is hungry, give him
　　bread to eat;
and if he is thirsty, give him
　　water to drink. . .
Do not rejoice when your enemy
　　falls,
and let not your heart be glad
　　when he stumbles."

"Love your enemies,
bless them that curse you.
Do good to them that hate you."

JOB 31.28–30

"I should have denied the God
    that is above,
if I rejoiced at the destruction
    of him that hated me,
or lifted up myself
    when evil found him.
Neither have I suffered my mouth to sin
    by wishing a curse
to his soul."

MATTHEW 5.44

"Love your enemies,
bless them that curse you.
Do good to them that hate you.
**And pray for them
which despitefully use you,
and persecute you.**"

JOB 36.5 . . . 25.3

"Behold, God is mighty,
    and does not despise any;
He is mighty in strength
    of understanding . . .
Upon whom does His light
    not arise?"

"Love your enemies,
    bless them that curse you.
Do good to them that hate you.
    And pray for them
which despitefully use you,
    and persecute you.
That you may be the children
    of your Father which is in heaven:
for He makes His sun to rise
    on the evil and the good,
and sends rain on the just
    and the unjust."

"For the Lord your God loves the stranger . .
   Therefore love the stranger . . .
Love him as yourself."

"For if you salute your brethren only,
what do you do more than others?"

LOVE YOUR ENEMIES – 2

PSALM 109.4–5

"Love your adversaries,
      make prayer for them,
though they reward you evil for good,
      and hatred for your love."

"Love your enemies,
pray for those
that persecute you."

AND HE TAUGHT THEM,
SAYING,

PROVERBS 6.24–25

"To keep you from
    your neighbor's wife,
from the smooth tongue
    of the adultress,
lust not
    in your heart
after her beauty."

"Everyone who looks at a woman
   lustfully,
has already committed adultery
   with her in his heart."

"Be you perfect. . .
   For I am the Lord your God,
and you shall be holy,
   for I am holy."

MATTHEW 5.48

"Be you therefore perfect,
   even as your Father
which is in heaven
   is perfect."

II Kings 4.32–35

"And when Elisha came into the house,
    the child was dead.
He went in therefore,
    and shut the door on
the mother and child,
    and prayed to the Lord.
Then the child opened his eyes."

"When you pray,
   enter your closet.
and when you have shut the door,
   pray to your Father in secret;
and your Father who sees in secret
   shall reward you openly."

PROVERB 23.4–5

"Labour not to be rich.
　For riches certainly
make themselves wings:
　they fly away
as an eagle toward heaven."

"Lay not up for yourself
    treasures upon earth,
where moth and rust corrupt,
    and where thieves
break through and steal.
    But lay up for yourself
treasures in heaven,
    where neither moth nor rust
does corrupt,
    and where thieves do not
break or steal."

"The Lord is my shepherd;
   I shall not want.
He makes me to lie down
   in green pastures;
He leads me beside the still waters.
   Yes, though I walk through
the valley of the shadow of death,
   I will fear no evil;
for You are with me.
   You prepare a table for me
in the presence of my enemies:
   You annoint my head with oil;
my cup runs over.
   Surely goodness and mercy
shall follow me
   all the days of my life:
and I will dwell in the house of
   the Lord forever."

"Therefore take no thought,
   saying, What shall we eat?
or, What shall we drink?
   or, Where shall we be clothed?
For your heavenly Father knows that
   you have need of all these things."

JOB 12.7–9

"Ask the birds of the air,
    and they will tell you;
or the plants of the earth,
    and they will teach you.
Who among all these
    does not know
that the hand of the Lord
    has done this?"

"Look at the birds of the air:
    They neither sow nor reap
nor gather into barns, and yet
    your heavenly Father feeds them.
Consider the lilies of the field:
    they neither toil nor spin;
yet I tell you, even Solomon
    in his glory was not arrayed
like one of those."

"I was ready to be sought
   by those who did not ask for me;
I was ready to be found
   by those who did not seek me . . .
I will open,
   and none shall shut."

"Ask, and it will be
given you;
seek, and you will
find;
knock, and it will be
opened to you."

"Like a father pities
    his children,
so the Lord pities them
    that fear Him. . .
Can a woman forget
    her suckling child,
that she should not have compassion
    on the son of her womb?
Yes, they may forget,
    yet I will not
forget you."

"What man is there of you,
   whom if his son ask bread,
will give him a stone?
   Or if he ask a fish,
will give him a serpent?
   If you then, being evil,
know how to give good gifts to
   your children,
how much more shall your Father
   which is in heaven
give good things to them that
   ask Him?"

"Behold, I set before you
    the way of life,
and the way
    of death. . .
I will cause you to walk
    in the straight way. . .
I will open to you
    the gates of righteousness. . .
For whoever finds Me,
    finds life;
But all that hate Me,
    love death."

MATTHEW 7.13

"Enter you in at the straight gate:
    for wide is the gate,
and broad is the way,
    that leads to destruction,
and many there are
    that go in that way.
Because straight is the gate,
    and narrow is the way,
which leads to life,
    and few there be
that find it."

"Even a child is known
by his doings,
whether his work is pure,
and whether it is right. . .
The fruit of the righteous
is a tree of life."

"You shall know them
   by their fruits.
Every good tree brings forth
   good fruit;
but a corrupt tree brings forth
   evil fruit."

"Who is wise, and
   will observe these things. . .
the Lord will be his strong rock,
   a house of defense to save him."

"Whosoever hears these sayings of mine,
and does them,
I will liken him to a wise man,
who builds his house upon a rock."

WHAT GOD ASKS
FROM BOTH RELIGIONS

ISAIAH 56.1

"Do justice,
    for My salvation
is near."

MATTHEW 4.17

"Repent,
   for the kingdom of heaven
is at hand."

ISAIAH 58.7

"Share your bread
    with the hungry,
and bring the homeless poor
    into your house;
when you see him naked,
    cover him."

"I was hungry
   and you gave me food,
I was a stranger
   and you welcomed me,
I was naked
   and you clothed me."

PSALM 37.14–15

"The wicked have drawn out the sword.
Their sword shall enter
into their own heart."

MATTHEW 27.52

**"All they that take the sword
shall perish by the sword."**

JOB 27.8

"For what is the hope of the hypocrite,
   though he has gained,
when God takes away his soul?"

MATTHEW 16.26

"For what is a man profited,
   if he shall gain the whole world,
and lose his own soul?"

PSALM 131.1–2

"O Lord, my heart is not proud,
    nor are my eyes haughty.
Nay, rather, I have stilled and
    quieted my soul
Like a weaned child.
    Like a weaned child
on its mother's lap."

"Except you be converted
    and become as little children,
you shall not enter into the
    kingdom of heaven.
Who therefore
    shall humble himself
as this little child,
    the same is greatest in the
kingdom of heaven."

"Who can say,
    I have made my heart clean,
I am pure from my sin?"

"He that is without sin
among you,
let him first cast a stone
at her."

"For the commandment is a lamp;
and the law is a light;
and the reproofs of instruction
are the way of life."

"And, behold, one came and said to him,
  'Good Master, what good thing shall I do
that I may have eternal life?'
  And he said to him. . .
**'If you will enter life,
  keep the commandments. . .' "**

PSALM 9.18

"The needy shall not always
be forgotten;
the hope of the poor
shall not perish forever."

"And, behold, one came and said to him,
    'Good Master, what good thing shall I do
that I may have eternal life?'
    And he said to him. . .
'If you will enter life,
    keep the commandments. . .
If you will be perfect,
    go and sell what you have,
and give to the poor. . .' "

PROVERB 16.18–19

"Pride goes before destruction.
    and a haughty spirit before a fall.
Better it is to be of
    a lowly spirit with the poor,
than divide the spoil with the proud."

"Verily, I say to you,
   that a rich man
shall hardly enter the kingdom of God."

DANIEL 3.44

"And the God of heaven
    shall set up a kingdom,
which shall never be destroyed:
    but shall stand for ever."

LUKE 10.9

"And heal the sick that
   are there within,
and say unto them:
   The kingdom of God
is come nigh to you."

THE NATURE OF THE HOLY
AND
THE POWER OF PRAYER

Numbers 6.24–27

"The Lord bless you,
   and keep you.
The Lord make His face
   shine upon you,
and be gracious
   to you.
The Lord lift up
   His countenance to you,
and give you peace."

JOHN 14.27

"Peace I leave with you,
   my peace I give to you;
not as the world gives,
   give I to you.
Let not your heart be troubled,
   neither let it be afraid."

JOB 42.2

**"I know that You
can do all things."**

**"With God
all things are possible."**

PSALM 37.4

"Delight in the lord,
  and He shall
give you
  the desires of
your heart."

"What things soever you desire,
when you pray,
believe that you receive them,
and you shall have them."

I<small>SAIAH</small> 56.5

"To them will I give
in My house
and within My walls
a place."

"In my Father's house
    are many mansions. . .
I go to prepare
    a place for you."

ISAIAH 56.6

"Also the sons of the stranger
    that join themselves to the Lord,
even them will I bring
    to My house of prayer."

JOHN 10.16

"And other sheep I have,
    which are not of this fold:
them also must I bring,
    and they shall hear my voice."

PSALM 55.22 . . . EXODUS 33.14

**"Cast your burden
on the Lord . . .
and He will give you rest."**

"Come unto me, all you that labor
and are heavily laden,
and I will give you rest."

"Who are you, that you should be afraid
    of a man who should die
and of a son of man
    who shall be made of grass? . . .
Do not be afraid of their faces;
    for I am with you
to deliver you."

"Do not be afraid of them
 that kill the body,
and after that have no more
 that they can do."

"You have delivered my soul
   from death. . .
You have destroyed death
   forever. . .
I shall not die,
   but live."

"For he is not a God of
the dead,
but of the living;
for all live to him."

"Your dead shall live.
   their corpses shall rise;
awake and sing,
   you who lie in the dust.
For your dew
   is the dew of light,
and the land of shades
   gives birth."

JOHN 5.29

"They shall come forth,
    they that have done good,
into the resurrection of life."

Isaiah 55.1-3

"Everyone who thirsts,
come to the waters.
Come to me, hear, and
your soul shall live."

John 4.14

"Whoever drinks of the water
   that I shall give him
shall never thirst;
   but the water that I
shall give to him
   shall be in him
a well of water
   springing up into
everlasting life."

Psalm 82.6

"You are gods;
　and all of you are
children of the most High."

JOHN 10.34

"You are gods."

"If the plague of the leper
    be healed,
then shall the priest command
    to take for him two birds;
and he shall sprinkle
    upon him seven times,
and shall pronounce him clean."

Jesus, to the healed leper:

"See you tell no man,
but go your way,
show yourself to the priest,
and offer the gift
that Moses commanded,
for a testimony to them."

HABAKKUK 2.4

**"The righteous shall live
by his faith."**

LUKE 17.19

Jesus to the healed Samaritan:

**"Your faith has made
you whole."**

"Then will I sprinkle
    clean water on you,
and you shall be clean.
    From all your filthiness,
and from all your idols,
    will I cleanse you."

"Now you are clean
through the word
I have spoken to you."

ISAIAH 51.22

"I have taken out of your hand
the cup of trembling,
you shall no more drink it
again."

Jesus speaking to God in the garden
of Gethsemane:

**"If this cup may not
    pass away from me,
except that I drink it,
    thy will be done."**

PSALM 31.5

"Into your hand
    I commit my spirit."

"Father, into your hands
   I commend my spirit."

ON THE HERITAGE OF INTERWEAVING
IN BIBLICAL WRITING

Biblical writers—in both the Hebrew scriptures and the New Testament
—searched the great writings that had come before them . . . took passages
from one after another of these writings . . . and then rewove them into
their new visions.

Jesus was one of a long line of prophets who used this method. The
Second Isaiah was an earlier example. Let us look now at one of his
interweavings.

Isaiah 58.14

"Then shall you delight yourself
   in the Lord;
and I will cause you to ride upon
   the high places of the earth,
and feed you with the heritage
   of Jacob, your father:
for the mouth of the Lord
   had spoken it."

Now let us look at the four earlier sources for this eight line verse.

In the current World Bible edition of the King James Version, there are listed in the center column five earlier references: Job 22.26 — Deuteronomy 32.13 and Deuteronomy 33.29 (which repeat each other) — Isaiah 1.20 — and Isaiah 40.5.

Since Isaiah 1.20 was written by First Isaiah, and is earlier than Second Isaiah, it can be used as a source. But, since Isaiah 40.5 and Isaiah 59.14 may be by the same author, I did not use Isaiah 40.5 as a source.

However, the concordance in this World Bible edition also links the word, 'feed', with Psalms 28.9. So this gives us four sources — one for each doublet of Isaiah 59.14.

Here are these four sources:

Job 22.26

"Then you shall have your delight
 in the Almighty,
and shall lift up your face to God."

Deuteronomy 32.13

"He made him ride on
 the high places of the earth,
that he might eat the increases
 of the fields;
and He made him to suck honey
 out of a rock,
and oil out of the flinty rock."

PSALM 28.9

"Save the people,
    and bless their inheritance:
feed them also,
    and lift them up for ever."

ISAIAH 1.20

"But if you refuse
    and rebel,
you shall be devoured
    with the sword.
For the mouth of the Lord
    had spoken it."

What Second Isaiah did was to weave passages together from these four sources to form his new verse. Here is the backbone of this new verse, using only the language of the original sources:

JOB 22.26. . . DEUTERONOMY 32.13. . . PSALM 28.9. . . ISAIAH 1.20

"Then you shall have your delight
    in the Almighty;
ride on
    the high places of the earth,
feed also
    their inheritance:
for the mouth of the Lord
    had spoken it."

And here again is the final verse: rounded out, incorporating his own terminology, and with personal references (in this verse, for example, "their" is changed to "you") brought in line with each other:

ISAIAH 59.14

"Then shall you delight yourself
    in the Lord;
and I will cause you to ride upon
    the high places of the earth,
and feed you
    with the heritage of Jacob, your father:
for the mouth of the Lord
    had spoken it."

It is especially important to note that Second Isaiah changed the entire context — and therefore the meaning — of the last two lines, even though he did not alter a single word in them. In the original, from Isaiah 1.20, the last two lines speak of rebellion and its subsequent destruction. However, in the new, interwoven Isaiah 59.14, the same last two lines speak of delight and triumph.

Jesus followed the same rules of reweaving: take from the hallowed past. . . join passages separated by time and space. . . sometimes reverse positive to negative, and negative to positive. . . express the same ideas by synonyms and parallel phraseologies. . . coordinate pronouns and personal references. . . establish new contexts and new meanings. . . ,etc.

He was doing nothing new in such reweaving, but was carrying on a great Biblical tradition.

LISTINGS OF INTERWEAVINGS
IN THE KING JAMES CENTER COLUMNS

For hundreds of years, of course, Christianity has recognized these interconnections between Jesus and the Hebrew Scriptures. In Psalms, Proverbs and Isaiah alone, there are 38 King James center column references to the four pages that make up Sermon on the Mount — Matthew 5, 6 and 7.

In addition, there are 22 unduplicated center column references reading back from the Sermon on the Mount to Psalms, Proverbs and Isaiah. This makes a total of 60 unduplicated cross-references to Psalms, Proverbs and Isaiah in the 111 verses that comprise the Sermon — about 2 references for every verse.

Some of these cross-references are to single phrases held in common between the Sermon and the Scriptures. But many of them are to multi-reference interweavings. And these continue throughout the entire New Testament.

For example, the King James center column points out the joining of Exodus 24.8 and Leviticus 17.11 in Matthew 26.28. As it does of Genesis 17.1 and Leviticus 11.44 in Matthew 6.48. As it does of Proverb 24.12 and Psalm 62.12 and Daniel 7.10 in Matthew 16.27.

ON THE CONTINUOUS RESTATEMENT
OF ETHICAL VALUES
IN THE HEBREW SCRIPTURES

In this book, I have left out many parallelisms between Jesus' statements and the Hebrew Scriptures that duplicated sources I already used.

You might wish to go through the Scriptures now, and find them for yourself. Here are just a few more.

1 KINGS 17.5-6/MATTHEW 6.11

"So he went and did according
    to the word of the Lord:
And the ravens brought him
    bread in the morning, and
bread in the evening."

PSALM 37.5/MATTHEW 6.31-32

"Commit your way to the Lord;
    trust also in Him;
and He shall bring it to pass."

JOB 31.1/MATTHEW 5.28

"I have made a covenant
    with my eyes;
why then should I think
    about a woman?"

PSALM 118.20/MATTHEW 7.14

"This gate of the Lord, into which
    the righteous shall enter."

JEREMIAH 31.9/MATTHEW 7.13-14

"They shall come with weeping, and
    with supplications will I lead them:
I will cause them to walk
    by the rivers of waters
in a straight way,
    wherein they shall not stumble."

ISAIAH 63.15-16/MATTHEW 6.9

"From heaven . . .
  You are our Father . . .
You, O Lord,
  are our Father,
our Redeemer . . .
  from everlasting."

JEREMIAH 32.17/MATTHEW 19.26

"Ah Lord God! Behold,
  there is nothing too hard for you."

PSALM 25.12-13/MATTHEW 5.5

"He that fears the Lord,
  his seed shall inherit the earth."

JEREMIAH 29.12-14/MATTHEW 7.7

"Then you shall call upon me,
   and I will hear you.
And you shall seek me,
   and find me.
And I will be found of you,
   saith the Lord."

HOSEA 13.14/JOHN 5.29

"I will ransom them from
   the power of the grave;
I will redeem them
   from death;
Oh death, I will be
   your plagues;
Oh graves, I will be
   your destruction."

OTHER HEBREW SOURCES FOR THE SAYINGS OF JESUS

I have also chosen only what I felt are the most moving of Jesus' sayings that come from the Hebrew Scriptures. But there are many more. For example:

Proverb 21.31. . . Luke 7.36
Isaiah 58.9. . . Mark 12.25
Psalm 79.12. . . Luke 6.38
Psalm 9.5-6. . . John 6.27
Proverb 14.31. . . Mark 26.40
Psalm 38.20. . . Mark 12.35
Leviticus 18.15. . . Luke 10.28
Proverb 20.6-7. . . Matthew 6.2-4
Ecclesiastes 5.2. . . Matthew 6.7
1 Kings 3.11-13. . . Matthew 7.33
Proverb 25.8. . . Matthew 5.25
Isaiah 28.16-18. . . Matthew 7.24
Isaiah 29.22-24. . . Mark 10.15
Deuteronomy 15.8-10. . . Luke 7.30
1 Kings 8.26-27. . . Matthew 6.10
Job 25.3. . . Matthew 5.45
Isaiah 58.5. . . Matthew 6.16
Proverbs 9.8 — 29.9. . . Matthew 7.6
Isaiah 58.9 . . . Proverb 8.17. . . Matthew 7.8
Leviticus 19.18. . . Matthew 7.12
Micah 3.5. . . Matthew 7.15
Psalm 102.25-26 . . . Jeremiah 18.18. . . Luke 16.17
Exodus 23.4-5. . . Luke 6.27
Proverbs 9.9-1.7. . . Matthew 13.12
Isaiah 42.18-20. . . Matthew 13.13
Psalm 37.5. . . Mark 11.23
Isaiah 60.21-22. . . Matthew 13.31
Proverbs 2.15 — 3.14-15. . . Matthew 13.44
Proverb 14.35. . . Matthew 24.25
Proverb 23.23. . . Matthew 14.45-46
Isaiah 25.6-8. . . John 13.49-50
2 Samuel 23.2. . . Matthew 10.20
Isaiah 51.6. . . Matthew 25.35
Numbers 6.24-27. . . John 14.27

2 Kings 8.11. . . John 11.35
Job 31.78. . . Matthew 5.29-30
Job 31.24. . . Mark 10.24
Isaiah 64.8. . . Matthew 6.9
Isaiah 43.18-19. . . Matthew 9.16-17
Isaiah 41.21–24. . . Matthew 13.18–23
Deuteronomy 15.7–8. . . Matthew 5.42
Proverb 11.25–27. . . 21.13. . . Matthew 7.1–2
Job 22.6–11. . . Matthew 25.41–42
Psalm 34.11. . . Mark 10.14
Isaiah 65.13–14. . . Luke 6.21–22
1 Kings 18.21. . . Matthew 6.24

Since the center columns and concordances of the King James version of the Bible were compiled many years ago, and since they were done by humans, rather than our more inclusive computers, I believe there must be even more. I would welcome any you may find in your own readings.

THE HEBREW SOURCES OF THE LORD'S PRAYER

This, again, is speculation.

Jesus — considered solely in his human aspect, as a rabbi, a sage — was perhaps the world's greatest poet. Like Homer, like Euripides, like Shakespeare, he took existing verses, and rewove them into immeasurable new depth and beauty.

This is especially true in The Lord's Prayer. It consists of nine short phrases, only sixty-six words. Yet Jesus uses them to encapsulate the great moments of previous Biblical history, and to give his own view of God the Father's relation to both Jew and Christian alike.

It seems evident that Jesus composed the Lord's Prayer so that it would have the same structure as his dialogue with the Jewish scribe in Mark 12.28-34. In both, he gives the essence of Judeo-Christianity as the willing obedience to the two great commandments: to love God without qualification, and to love your neighbor without qualification.

In the Lord's Prayer, he leads us daily to a deeper understanding of both these essential commandments, and their source in God the Father. He does this by calling upon the towering figures in Biblical history, and causing us to remember how they embraced each of these commands.

Remember, of course, that Jesus was speaking to two audiences simultaneously. The first was a small but vital audience of learned Jews, such as the scribe in Mark 12, who were as familiar with Scriptures as Jesus himself was. This audience would recognize immediately the full sources through which Jesus spoke.

The second audience, even more important to Jesus' goals, was far larger. It was those Jews who did not have the scholar's knowledge of the Scriptures, but still must be linked in prayer to God the Father.

And then, of course, his audience slowly swelled to the non-Jews, who knew little or nothing about Scriptures.

Therefore, his Lord's Prayer must reach all these audiences, from the most naive to the most learned. To the naive, it would talk solely about this moment, and their personal and spiritual needs of this moment. But to the learned, it would take on layer after layer of historical and spiritual depth.

Let us look at the Prayer as Jesus, and the scribe in Mark 12, might have seen it.

Jesus begins by calling upon King David. For it was David who first defined God as, **"Our Father. . . in the heaven"**. (1 Chronicles 29.10-11) And Jesus reaffirms that definition with, **"Our Father which art in heaven"**.

Jesus next turns to the question, "What does God the Father first ask from us?" And he answers this by bidding the one who prays to honor the first commandment, in this form:

"**My holy name...will be hallowed**". (Leviticus 22.32) And the pray-er replies, with Jesus, "**Hallowed be thy name**".

Then Jesus reminds us of how God would have us act to hallow his name: "**You shall be to me a kingdom of priests and a holy nation**". (Exodus 19.6.) And the pray-er replies, with Jesus, "**Thy kingdom come**".

Then Jesus reminds us what the result will be when we are a holy nation. To do this, he calls on Solomon, who, when he first brought the ark into the Temple, asked and answered, "**But will God dwell with men on earth? Behold, heaven cannot contain thee**". (2 Chronicles 6.18.) And Jesus reaffirms Solomon's faith in the final coming of God's kingdom, "**Thy will be done on earth, as it is in heaven**".

Then Jesus reminds us of what that world kingdom will hold for each of us. To do this, he calls on Moses, who assured his starving people who dared into the desert for God: "**In the morning, you shall be filled with bread**". (Exodus 16.12.) And Jesus promises that if the pray-er dares enough for God, he may join in the request, "**Give us this day our daily bread**".

Then Jesus turns to the question, "What is the second act God asks from us?" And he answers this by calling on Joseph, who, when his brothers begged him, "**Forgive the trespasses of your brethren**", replied, "**Fear not, I will nourish you**". (Genesis 50.16-21) And Jesus leads us, by Joseph's example, to nourish, without exception, all our brothers and sisters. And this allows the pray-er to then ask, "**Forgive our trespasses, as we forgive those who trespass against us**".

And then Jesus points out the great hidden barrier to the kingdom, by reminding us that, "**God did tempt Abraham, and said . . . 'Take now your only son, Isaac, and offer him for a burnt offering'.**" (Genesis 22.1.) And Jesus points out that Abraham did not give way to that ultimate temptation of doubting God's redemption. And Jesus confirms the terrible struggle against doubt that all of us must pass through by holding fast to faith in this crucifying world. And he leads the pray-er to ask our Father, **"And deliver us not into temptation"**.

And then Jesus calls on Job, from whom all had seemingly been taken, and who had also been tempted by monumental doubt, and who had then been redeemed by God for his final acceptance and faith — and to whom it was said, **"The Almighty shall deliver you. No evil shall touch you"**. (Job 5.17-19) And Jesus expresses his own acceptance and faith — and our acceptance and faith — with these words of unconquerable assurance in God's gift of salvation, **"But deliver us from evil"**.

And, having completed that circle of faith and prayer — Jesus returns to David the King, and the bond David first built between earth and heaven, when he affirmed, **"For ever, thine. . . is the power, and the glory, and. . . the kingdom"**. (1 Chronicles 29.10 11.)

And Jesus reaffirms almost these exact same words as **"For thine is the kingdom, and the power, and the glory, forever"**.

Now go on to read the full scriptural sources that Jesus used to compose this Prayer. There again, additional layers of meaning emerge. Jesus, by making present Isaac's willingness to be offered, confronts his own ultimate offering. And, in the passage from Job, this appears: **"Despise not the chastening of the Almighty: for He maketh sore, and bindeth up; He woundeth, and His hands make whole"**.

THE OLDER LEVELS OF THE BEATITUDES

Throughout the Beatitudes, Jesus was quite careful to refer his listeners back to well–marked passages in the Hebrew scriptures.

This gave him the ability to point out, through these subtexts, the strength that meekness requires. . . that righteousness delivers from death. . . that God gives us what we give each other . . . that the pure in heart shall see God from renewed flesh. . . that it is through peace alone that both Jew and Christian become the children of God. . . that the final reward of these actions of the Beatitudes is God Himself.

Here is an abbreviated sampling.

MATTHEW 5.5

"Blessed are the meek,
    for they shall inherit the earth."

PSALM 37.8-11

"Cease from anger, and forsake wrath:
    fret not yourself in any way to do evil.
For evildoers shall be cut off,
    but those who wait upon the Lord
shall inherit the earth.
    For in a little while, the wicked shall not be:
but *the meek shall inherit the earth;*
    and shall delight themselves
in the abundance of peace."

MATTHEW 5.6

"Blessed are they which
    do hunger and thirst after righteousness:
for they shall be filled."

Proverb 10.2–3

"Treasures of wickedness profit nothing:
    but righteousness delivers from death.
The lord will not suffer the soul
    of the righteous to famish."

PSALM 104.28–30

"You open Your hand,
    they are filled with good . . .
You send forth Your spirit,
    they are created:
and You renew the face of the earth."

MATTHEW 5.7

"Blessed are merciful,
    for they shall obtain mercy."

PSALM 18.24–28

"Therefore has the Lord recompensed me
   according to my righteousness,
according to the cleanliness of my hands
   in His eyesight.
*With the merciful You will show
   Yourself merciful;*
with the upright man, You will show
   Yourself upright;
with the pure, You will show
   Yourself pure;
and with the froward, You will show
   Yourself froward."

MATTHEW 5.8

"Blessed are the pure in heart,
   for they shall see God"

PSALM 24.4–5

"*He who has* clean hands and *a pure heart,*
   who does not lift up his soul

to what is false. . .
  he will receive a blessing from the Lord."

Job 19.25–27

"For I know that my Redeemer lives,
  and that at last
He will stand upon the earth;
  and after my skin has been destroyed,
then from my flesh I *shall see God.*

Matthew 5.9

"Blessed are the peacemakers,
  for they shall be called sons of God."

Isaiah 32.12–18

And *the work of righteousness shall be peace;*
  and the effect of righteousness
quietness and assurance forever.
  And My people shall dwell in a
peaceable habitation, and in sure dwellings,
  and in quiet resting places."

HOSEA 1.10

"And it shall come to pass,
   that in the place where it was said to them,
'You are not My people',
   there *it shall be said to them,*
'*You are the sons of* the living *God*'."

MATTHEW 5.12

"Rejoice, and be exceedingly glad,
   for great is your reward in heaven."

ISAIAH 66.10–13

"*Rejoice* with Jerusalem, *and be glad* with her,
   all you who love her:
rejoice with joy for her,
   all you that mourn for her . . .
Behold, I will extend peace to her like a river,
   and the glory of the Gentiles like a flowing stream."

"The word of the Lord came to Abram in a vision,
  saying,
'Fear not, Abram, *I am* your shield,
  and your *exceeding great reward* . . .
Look now toward heaven, and number the stars,
  if you are able to number them.'
And He said to Abram,
  'So shall your seed be'."

HOW FAR WAS THE SCRIBE
FROM THE KINGDOM OF GOD?

Throughout this book, as you have seen, Jesus talked in code — in a second, deeper message that could be heard only by those who knew the Hebraic sources of his words. And, in the meeting with the scribe, the scribe responded to him in a similar code:

MARK 12.32

"You are right, Teacher;
  you have truly said that He is one,
and there is no other but He;
  and to love Him with all your heart,
and with all your understanding,
  and with all your strength,

and to love your neighbor as yourself,
   is much more than all the whole
burnt offerings and sacrifices."

What the scribe was referring to, and what Jesus immediately understood, was a vision that had run through Judaism for close to a thousand years:

1 Samuel 15.22

"Has the Lord as great a delight
   in burnt offering and sacrifices,
as in obeying
   the voice of the Lord?
Behold, to obey is better than sacrifice,
   and to hearken than the fat of lambs."

Hosea 6.6

"For I desire steadfast love
   and not sacrifice,
the knowledge of God rather than
   burnt offerings."

Micah 6.6

" 'With what shall I come before the Lord,
   and bow myself before God on high?

Shall I come before Him with burnt offerings,
    with calves a year old?
Will the Lord be pleased with thousands of rams,
    with ten thousands of rivers of oil?
Shall I give my first-born
    for my transgression,
the fruit of my body
    for the sin of my soul?'
He has showed you, O man, what is good;
    and what does the Lord require of you
but to do justice, and to love kindness,
    and to walk humbly with your God."

And when Jesus heard what the scribe said, and recalled its echos through almost a thousand years, he knew that he had been heard and understood. And his reply was this:

MARK 12.34

"You are not far
    from the Kingdom of God."

But his deeper reference was this:

ISAIAH 46.13

"I will bring near My deliverance,
    it is not far off,
and My salvation will not tarry."

For Jesus and the scribe agreed that it was love — practiced daily as the obedience to God that required justice and kindness to men and women — that would bring salvation for the Jew, and the Kingdom of God for the Christian.

THE ORIGINALITY AND UNIQUENESS OF JESUS' VISION

This, again, is the speculation. And, once again, I speak only of Jesus in his human aspect.

From the beginning of his life to the end of his life, Jesus believed that the universal love of human for human would be the indispensible requirement for the universal realization of God's kingdom. The giving of this love was the recurrent theme of the Sermon on the Mount, the Lord's Prayer, the Beatitudes, the meeting with the scribe, and so much more that we have been witness to in this book.

But Jesus also knew that humans, through their own powers, could not live the Sermon on the Mount. That humans, through their own powers, could not carry out the doctrine of perfection. That man — even Jesus as man — is by his inherited nature incapable of the highest good:

MATTHEW 19. 16-17

"And, behold, one came and said to him,

'Good Master, what good thing shall I do that I may have eternal life?'

And he said to him,

'Why do you call me good?

There is none good but one,

that is, God:

**but if you will enter into life,
keep the commandments:"**

ECCLESIASTES 12-13. . . 8.20

**"Fear God and keep His commandments,
    for this is the whole duty of man. . .
For there is not a just man upon earth,
    that does good, and sins not."**

And his vision seems to have been least partially this: that Jesus, as man, as the Son of Man, must pass through the cross, and give himself as Job's ransom for man's sins.

MARK 10.45

**"For even the Son of Man
    came to give his life
as a ransom for the life of many."**

JOB 33.23-28

**"If there be an angel,
    a mediator. . .
to declare to man what is right for him:
    and he is gracious to him, and says,
'Deliver him from going down into the pit,
    I have found a ransom. . .'**

Then man prays to God, and He accepts him,
   he comes into His presence with joy;
he recounts to men his salvation,
   and he sings before men and says,
'I sinned and perverted what was right,
   and it was not requited to me.
He has redeemed my soul
   from going down into the pit,
and my life shall see the light'."

JOB 36.18

"Let not the greatness of the ransom turn you aside."

The Messiah, of course, was already anticipated in Judaism. But the Son of Man, as conceived by Jesus, was by no means the expected Messiah. For the Messiah would prove to be invulnerable, and would come to rule the world — in a single lifetime alone — in triumph and glory.

Therefore, Jesus let it be known, through the contrast between what he said, and its source in the Hebraic Scriptures, that his first coming would be exactly the opposite of the Messiah's:

JOHN 10.11

"I am the good shepherd;
   the good shepherd gives his life
for the sheep."

EZEKIEL 34.31

"You are my flock,
   the flock of my pasture are men,
and I am your God."

MATTHEW 23.11

"He that is greatest among you
   shall be your servant. . . "

ISAIAH 53.11-12

"By his knowledge
   shall My righteous servant justify many;
for he shall bear
   their iniquities.
Therefore will I divide
   him a portion with the great. . .
because he has poured out his soul unto death:
   and he was numbered with

the transgressors;
   and he bare the sin of many,
and made intercession for the transgressors."

And, time and time again, Jesus incorporated his new vision into the Scriptural language he had been given:

EZEKIEL 34. 14-16

"The Lord God will seek that
   which was lost,
and bring again that
   which was driven away."

MATTHEW 18.11

"For the Son of Man is come
   to save that which is lost."

PSALM 26.8

"Good and upright is the Lord:
   therefore will He teach sinners
in the way."

LUKE 6.32

"I came not to call the righteous,
   but sinners
to repentence."

This language was familiar and revered. But now, in Jesus' hands, it was restructured to create something completely new in the history of the entire — and not just the Jewish — world. There had been gods in other cultures who had been killed and reborn — but for what purpose? Not for universal justice and universal redemption and universal immortality!

The ethical uniqueness of Judaism was retained in its new sibling religion. In both, love was the core of the two great commands. Love for your neighbor, love for the stranger, love for all of God's children.

This was the first essence. The second was love for God, and for God's liberator of the world. In Judaism, he is known as the Messiah, and we still await his first coming. In Jesus' younger religion, he is known as the Christ, and we still await his second coming.

But we wait. . . and love. . . together.

THE REFERENCES USED

In addition to the King James Bible and its concordance, I have used the Protestant New Oxford Annotated Bible, and the Catholic New American Bible.

I have checked each source in all three of them. Each, of course, varies from the others in many of these translations. Therefore, since no one knows the correlation between the text Jesus used and the sources used by any later bible, I have felt free to use any of the three bibles for any particular passage.

Also, since nearly all prayer books and missals I have seen use the Tyndale 'trespasses' in Matthew 6.12, as well as 6.14 and 15, I have kept this usage.

THE FULL TEXTS OF THE JEWISH SOURCES

For each quote, I give first the page number, then the source — either the King James Bible (KJ), the New Oxford Annotated Bible (OA), or the New American Bible (NA) — and then the full quote. In only one case, page 76, I have replaced a line in the King James Bible with the same line in the Oxford Annotated, since the latter fills out the meaning of that line.

It is imperative, of course, that you compare the full text of each source with its re-presentation in the front of the book. And I suggest that you also read the entire verse surrounding it to understand its full context.

Page 2.   (KJ) LEVITICUS 19.18 "You shall not take vengeance or bear any grudge against the sons of your own people, **but you shall love your neighbor as yourself:** I am the LORD."

Page 4.   (OA) DEUTERONOMY 6.4 **"Hear, O Israel; The LORD our God is one LORD,** and you shall love the LORD your God with all your heart, and with all your soul, and with all your might."

Page 6.   (OA) DEUTERONOMY 6.5 "Hear, O Israel; the LORD our God is one LORD; and **you shall love the LORD your God with all your heart, and with all your soul, and with all your might.**"

Page 13.   (OA) ISAIAH 52.7 **"How beautiful upon the mountains are the feet of him who brings good tidings, who publishes peace, who brings good tidings of good, who publishes salvation, who says to Zion, 'Your God reigns'."**

Page 16.   (KJ) PSALM 32.2 **"Blessed is the man** unto whom the Lord imputeth not iniquity, and in whose spirit there is no guile."

(KJ) ISAIAH 66.2 "For all those things hath Mine hand made, and all those things have been, saith the LORD: but to this man will I look, even to him **that is poor** and **of** a contrite **spirit**, and trembleth at my word."

(KJ) ISAIAH 57.15 "For thus saith the high and lofty one that inhabiteth eternity, whose name is Holy, '**I dwell in the high and holy place with him** also that is of a contrite and humble spirit, to revive the spirit of the humble, and to revive the heart of the contrite ones'."

Page 18.   (OA) ISAIAH 61.1-2 **"The Spirit of the Lord GOD is upon me,** because the LORD has anointed me to bring good tidings to the afflicted, he has sent me to bind up the brokenhearted, to proclaim liberty to the captives, and the opening of the prison to those who are bound, to proclaim the year of the LORD'S favor, and the day of vengeance of our God; **to comfort all who mourn."**

Page 20.   (KJ) PSALM 37.11 **"The meek shall inherit the earth;** and shall delight themselves in the abundance of peace."

Page 22.   (KJ) PSALMS 107:5-9 **"Hungry and thirsty, their soul fainted in them.** Then they cried unto the LORD in their trouble, and he delivered them out of their distresses. **And he led them forth by the right way,** that they might go to a city of habitation. Oh that men would praise the LORD for his goodness, and for his wonderful works to the children of men! For he satisfieth the longing soul, **and filleth the hungry soul with goodness."**

Page 24.   (KJ) PSALM 18.25 **"With the merciful thou wilt shew thyself merciful;** with an upright man thou wilt shew thyself upright."

Page 26.　(OA) PSALM 24.4-5 **"He who has** clean hands and **a pure heart**, who does not lift up his soul to what is false, and does not swear deceitfully."

　　　　(OA) JOB 19.26 "And after my skin has been thus destroyed, then from my flesh I **shall see God.**"

Page 28.　(KJ) ISAIAH 32.17 "And **the work of righteousness shall be peace;** and the effect of righteousness quietness and assurance forever."

　　　　(OA) HOSEA 1.10 "The number of the children of Israel shall be as the sand of the sea, which cannot be measured or numbered; and it shall come to pass, that in the place where it was said to them, 'You are not My people', there **it shall be said to them, 'You are the sons of the living God'.**"

Page 30.　(OA) ISAIAH 51.7-8 **"Hearken to me, you who know righteousness,** the people in whose heart is my law; **fear not the reproach of men, and be not dismayed at their revilings.** For the moth will eat them up like a garment, and the worm will eat them like wool; but **my deliverance will be for ever**, and my salvation to all generations."

Page 32.　(KJ) ISAIAH 66.10 **"Rejoice** with Jerusalem, **and be glad** with her, all you who love her: rejoice with joy for her, all you that mourn for her."

　　　　(KJ) GENESIS 15.1 "The word of the Lord came to Abram in a vision, saying, 'Fear not, Abram, **I am** your shield, and **your exceeding great reward . . .** "

Page 36.　(KJ) I CHRONICLES 29.10-11 "Wherefore David blessed the LORD before all the congregation; and David said, 'Blessed be thou, LORD God of Israel **our Father,** for ever and ever. Thine, O LORD, is the greatness, and the power, and the glory, and the victory, and the majesty; for all that is **in the heaven** and in the earth is thine; thine is the kingdom, O LORD, and thou art exalted as head above all'."

Page 38.   (OA) LEVITICUS 22.32 "And you shall not profane **my holy name**, but I **will be hallowed** among the people of Israel; I am the LORD who sanctify you."

Page 40.   (NA) EXODUS 19.6 **"You shall be unto me a kingdom of priests, a holy nation.** This is what you must tell the Israelites."

Page 42.   (KJ) 2 CHRONICLES 6:18 **"But will God** in very deed **dwell with men on** the **earth? behold, heaven** and the heaven of heavens **cannot contain thee;** how much less this house which I have built!"

Page 44.   (KJ) EXODUS 16:12 "I have heard the murmurings of the children of Israel; speak unto them, saying, At even ye shall eat flesh, and **in the morning ye shall be filled with bread; and ye shall know that I am the LORD your God."**

Page 46.   (KJ) GENESIS 50:17-21 **"So shall ye say unto Joseph,** Forgive, I pray thee now, **the trespass of thy brethren,** and their sin; for they did unto thee evil: and now, we pray thee, **forgive the trespass of the servants of the God of thy father.** And Joseph wept when they spake unto him. And his brethren also went and fell down before his face; and they said, 'Behold, we be thy servants'. **And Joseph said unto them,** 'Fear not; for am I in the place of God? But as for you, ye thought evil against me; but God meant it unto good, to bring to pass, as it is this day, to save much people alive. Now therefore fear ye not; **I will nourish you,** and your little ones'. And he comforted them, and spake kindly unto them."

Page 48.   (KJ) GENESIS 22.1-2 **"And it came to pass** after these things, **that God did tempt Abraham, and said** unto him, Abraham: and he said, Behold, here I am. And he said, **Take now** thy son, **thine only son Isaac,** whom thou lovest, and get thee into the land of Mori-ah; **and offer him** there for **a burnt offering** upon one of the mountains which I will tell thee of."

Page 50.   (OA) JOB 5.17-19 "Behold, happy is the man whom God reproves; therefore despise not the chastening of **the Almighty,** For he wounds, but he binds up; he smites, but his hands heal, He **will deliver you from** six troubles; in seven no **evil** shall touch you."

Page 52.   (KJ) I CHRONICLES 29.10-11 "Wherefore David blessed the LORD before all the congregation; and David said, Blessed be thou, LORD God of Israel our father, **for ever** and ever. **Thine,** O LORD, **is** the greatness, and **the power, and the glory, and the** victory, and the majesty; for all that is in the heaven and in the earth is thine; thine is the **kingdom,** O LORD, and thou art exalted as head above all."

Page 56.   (NA) PROVERB 24.29 **"Say not, 'as he did to me, so will I do to him; I will repay the man according to his deeds'."**

Page 58.   (OA) PROVERB 20.22 **"Do not say, 'I will repay evil';** wait for the LORD, and he will help you."

(KJ) LAMENTATIONS 3.30 **"He giveth his cheek to him that smiteth him;** he is filled with reproach."

Page 60.   (OA) EXODUS 23.4-5 **"If you meet your enemy's ox or his ass going astray, you shall bring it back to him. If you see the ass of him that hates you lying under its burden, you shall refrain from leaving him with it, and you shall help him lift it up."**

Page 62.   (KJ) 2 SAMUEL 19:6 "In that thou **lovest thine enemies,** and hatest thy friends. For thou hast declared this day, that thou regardest neither princes nor servants: for this day I perceive, that if Absalom had lived, and all we had died this day, then it had pleased thee well."

Page 64.   (OA) PSALMS 109:28-29 **"Let them curse, but bless thou:** when they arise, let them be ashamed; but let thy servant rejoice. Let mine adversaries be clothed with shame, and let them cover themselves with their own confusion, as with a mantle."

Page 66.   (OA) PROVERB 25.21 **"If your enemy is hungry, give him bread to eat; and if he is thirsty, give him water to drink."**

(OA) PROVERB 24.17 **"Do not rejoice when your enemy falls, and let not your heart be glad when he stumbles."**

Page 68.   (KJ)JOB 31.28-30 "This also were an iniquity to be punished by the judge; for **I should have denied the God that is above, if I rejoiced at the destruction of him that hated me, or lifted up myself when evil found him. Neither have I suffered my mouth to sin by wishing a curse to his soul."**

Page 70.   (OA) JOB 36.5 **"Behold, God is mighty, and does not despise any; He is mighty in strength of understanding."**

(KJ) JOB 25.3 "Is there any number of his armies? and **upon whom doth not his light arise?"**

Page 72.   (KJ) DEUTERONOMY 10.17-20 **"For the Lord your God** is a God of Gods, and a Lord of lords, a great God, a mighty, and a terrible, Which regardeth not persons, nor taketh reward. He doth execute the judgment of the fatherless and widow, and **loveth the stranger** in giving him food and raiment. **Love Ye therefore the stranger;** for ye were strangers in the land of Egypt.

(KJ) LEVITICUS 19.34 "But the stranger that dwelleth within you shall be unto you as one born among you, and thou shall **love him as yourself;** for you were strangers in the land of Egypt: I am the Lord your God."

Page 76.   (KJ) PSALM 109. 4-5 "For my **Love,** they are **my adversaries,** (OA) even as **I make prayer for them. So they reward me evil for good, and hatred for my love."**

Page 80. (NA) PROVERB 6.24-25 **"To keep you from your neighbor's wife, from the smooth tongue of the adulteress, lust not in your heart after her beauty;** let her not captivate you with her glance."

Page 82. (KJ) GENESIS 17.1 "And when Abram was ninety years old and nine, the Lord appeared to Abram, and said unto him, 'I am the Almighty God; walk before me; and **thou be perfect'."**

(KJ) LEVITICUS 11.44 **"For I am the LORD your God:** ye shall therefore sanctify yourselves, **and ye shall be holy; for I am holy:** neither shall ye defile yourselves with any manner of creeping thing that creepeth upon the earth."

Page 84. (KJ) II KINGS 4.32-35 **"And when E-li-sha was come into the house,** behold, **the child was dead,** and laid upon his bed. **He went in therefore, and shut the door upon them twain, and prayed unto the LORD.** And he went up, and lay upon the child, and put his mouth upon his mouth, and his eyes upon his eyes, and his hands upon his hands: and he stretched himself upon the child; and the flesh of the child waxed warm. **Then** he returned, and walked in the house to and fro; and went up, and stretched himself upon him; and the child sneezed seven times, and **the child opened his eyes."**

Page 86. (KJ) PROVERB 23.4-5 **"Labour not to be rich:** cease from thine own wisdom. Wilt thou set thine eyes upon that which is not? **for riches certainly make themselves wings; they fly away as an eagle toward heaven."**

Page 88. (KJ) PSALM 23.1-6 **"The LORD is my shepherd; I shall not want. He maketh me to lie down in green pastures; he leadeth me beside the still waters. He restoreth my soul: he leadeth me in the paths of righteousness for his name's sake. Yea, though I walk through the valley of the shadow of death, I will fear no evil; for thou art with me; thy rod and thy staff they comfort me. Thou preparest** a table before me in the presence of mine enemies: thou anointest my head with oil; my cup runneth over. **Surely goodness and mercy shall follow me all the days of my life: and I will dwell in the house of the LORD forever."**

Page 90.   (OA) JOB 12.7-9 **"But ask the** beasts, and they will teach you; the **birds of the air, and they will tell you. Or the plants of the earth, and they will teach you;** and the fish of the sea will declare to you. **Who among all these does not know that the hand of the LORD has done this?"**

Page 92.   (OA) ISAIAH 65.1 **"I was ready to be sought by those who did not ask for me; I was ready to be found by those who did not seek me.** I said, 'Here am I, here am I,' to a nation that did not call on my name."

(OA) ISAIAH 22.22 "And the key of the house of David **I** will lay upon his shoulder; so he shall **open, and none shall shut;** and he shall shut, and none shall open."

Page 94.   (KJ) PSALM 103.13 **"Like as a father pitieth his children, so the LORD pitieth them that fear him."**

(KJ) ISAIAH 49.15 **"Can a woman forget her sucking child, that she should not have compassion on the son of her womb? yea, they may forget, yet will I not forget thee."**

Page 96.   (KJ) JEREMIAH 21.8 "And to the people you shall say, 'Thus says the Lord: **Behold, I set before you the way of life, and the way of death'."**

(KJ) JEREMIAH 31.9 **"I will cause you to walk in the straight way."**

(KJ) PSALM 118.19 **"Open to me the gates of righteousness:** I will go into them, and I will praise the Lord."

(KJ) PROVERB 8.35-36 **"For all who find me find life,** and shall obtain the favor of the Lord. **But** he that sins against Me wrongs his own soul: **all they that hate Me love death."**

Page 98.　(KJ) PROVERB 20.11 **"Even a child is known by** his **doings, whether his work be pure, and whether it be right."**

(KJ) PROVERB 12.30 **"The fruit of the righteous is a tree of life;** and he that wins souls is wise."

Page 100.　(KJ) PSALM 107.43 **"Whoso is wise, and will observe these things,** even they shall understand the loving-kindness of the Lord."

(KJ) PSALM 31.1-2 "In You, O Lord, I put my trust; let me never be ashamed: deliver me in my righteousness. Bow down Your ear to me; deliver me speedily; **be You my strong rock,** for a **house of defense** to save me."

Page 104. (KJ) ISAIAH 56.1　"Thus saith the LORD, Keep ye judgment, and **do justice: for my salvation is near** to come, and my righteousness to be revealed."

Page 106. (OA) ISAIAH 58.7 "Is it not to **share your bread with the hungry, and bring the homeless poor into your house; when you see him naked,** to **cover him,** and not to hide yourself from your own flesh?"

Page 108. (KJ) PSALM 37.14-15 **"The wicked have drawn out the sword,** and have bent their bow, to cast down the poor and needy, and to slay such as be of upright conversation. **Their sword shall enter into their own heart,** and their bows shall be broken."

Page 110. (KJ) JOB 27.8 **"For what is the hope of the hypocrite, though he has gained, when God takes away his soul?"**

Page 112. (KJ) PSALM 131.1-2 **"LORD, my heart is not haughty, nor mine eyes lofty:** neither do I exercise myself in great matters, or in things too high for me. **Surely I have behaved and quieted myself, as a child that is weaned of his mother: my soul is even as a weaned child."**

Page 114. (OA) PROVERB 20.9 **"Who can say, 'I have made my heart clean; I am pure from my sin?' "**

Page 116. (KJ) PROVERB 7.23 **"For the commandment is a lamp; and the law is a light; and the reproofs of instruction are the way of life."**

Page 118. (OA) PSALM 9.18 **"For the needy shall not always be forgotten; and the hope of the poor shall not perish forever."**

Page 120. (OA) PROVERB 16.18-19 **"Pride goes before destruction, and a haughty spirit before a fall. It is better to be of a lowly spirit with the poor, than divide the spoil with the proud."**

Page 122. (KJ) DANIEL 3.44 **"And** in the days of these kings, **shall the God of heaven set up a kingdom, which shall never be destroyed:** and the kingdom shall not be left to other people, **but** shall break into pieces and consume all these kingdoms, and it **shall stand for ever."**

Page 126. (OA) NUMBERS 6.24–27 **"The Lord bless you, and keep you. The Lord make His face shine upon you, and be gracious to you. The Lord lift up His countenance to you, and give you peace."**

Page 128. (OA) JOB 42.4 **"I know that you can do all things,** and that no purpose of yours can be thwarted."

Page 130. (OA) PSALM 37.4 "Take **delight in the LORD; and He will give thee the desires of thine heart."**

Page 132. (KJ) ISAIAH 56.5 "Even **unto them will I give in Mine house and within My walls a place** and a name better than of sons and of daughters: I will give them an everlasting name, that shall not be cut off."

Page 134. (KJ) ISAIAH 56.6 **"Also the sons of the stranger, that join themselves to the LORD,** to serve him, and to love the name of the LORD, to be his servants, every one that keepeth the sabbath from polluting it, and taketh hold of my covenant; **even them will I bring to** my holy mountain, and make them joyful in **my house of prayer:** their burnt offerings and their sacrifices shall be accepted upon mine altar; for mine house shall be called an house of prayer for all people."

Page 136. (OA) PSALM 55.22 **"Cast your burden on the Lord,** and He shall sustain you."

(OA) EXODUS 33.14 "And He said, My presence shall go with thee, **and I will give thee rest."**

Page 138. (KJ) ISAIAH 51.12. "I, even I, am he that comforteth you; **who art thou, that thou shouldest be afraid of a man that shall die, and of the son of man which shall be made as grass."**

(OA) JEREMIAH 1.8 **"Be not afraid** of them; **for I am with you to deliver you,** saith the LORD."

Page 140. (KJ) PSALM 56.13 **"For thou hast delivered my soul from death;** wilt not thou deliver my feet from falling, that I may walk before God in the light of the living?"

(NA) ISAIAH 28.7 "On this mountain He will destroy the veil that veils all peoples, the web that is woven over all nations; **He will destroy death forever.**"

(OA) PSALM 118.17 **"I shall not die, but** I shall **live,** and recount the deeds of the LORD."

Page 142. (NA) ISAIAH 26.19 **"But your dead shall live,** their corpses shall rise; **awake and sing, you who lie in the dust. For your dew is a dew of light, and the land of shades gives birth.**"

Page 144. (KJ) ISAIAH 55.1-3 "Ho, **every one that thirsteth, come ye to the waters,** and he that hath no money; come ye, buy, and eat; yea, come, buy wine and milk without money and without price. Wherefore do ye spend money for that which is not bread? and your labour for that which satisfieth not? hearken diligently unto me, and eat ye that which is good, and let your soul delight itself in fatness. Incline your ear, and **come unto me: hear, and your soul shall live;** and I will make an everlasting covenant with you, even the sure mercies of David."

Page 146. (OA) PSALM 82.6 "I say, **You are gods; and all of you are children of the Most High.**"

Page 148. (KJ) LEVITICUS 14.3-7 "This shall be the law of the leper in the day of his cleansing: He shall be brought unto the priests: And the priest shall go forth out of the camp; and the priest shall look, and, behold, **if the plague of leprosy be healed in the leper; then shall the priest command to take for him** that is to be cleansed **two birds** alive and clean, and cedar wood, and scarlet, and hyssop: and the priest shall command that one of the birds be killed in an earthen vessel over running water: as for the living bird, he shall take it, and the cedar wood, and the scarlet, and the hyssop, and shall dip them and the living bird in the blood of the bird that was killed over the running water: **and he shall sprinkle upon him** that is to be cleansed from the leprosy **seven times, and shall pronounce him clean,** and shall let the living bird loose into the open field."

Page 150. (OA) HABAKKUK 2.4 "Behold, **he whose his soul is not upright** in him **shall fail, but the righteous shall live by his faith."**

Page 152. (KJ) EZEKIEL 36.25 **"Then will I sprinkle clean water upon you, and ye shall be clean: from all your filthiness, and from all your idols, will I cleanse you."**

Page 154. (KJ) ISAIAH 51.22 "Thus saith thy Lord the LORD, and thy God that pleadeth the cause of his people, Behold, **I have taken out of thine hand the cup of trembling,** even the dregs of the cup of my fury: **thou shalt no more drink it again."**

Page 156. (OA) PSALM 31.5 **"Into thine hand I commit my spirit:** thou has redeemed me, O LORD, faithful God."

GIVE THE GIFT OF THIS JEWISH-CHRISTIAN BROTHERHOOD TO YOUR FRIENDS

ORDER FORM

Please send _____copies of You are not far from the Kingdom of God at $19.98. (New York residents please include sales tax.)

$ _____Check/MO enclosed

Name _____

Company _____

Address _____

City/State/Zip _____

Phone ( ) _____

❏ Please send me more information about your other materials on Judeo-Christianity.

Check your leading bookstore.

Second Creation Press
210 East 86th Street, Suite 501
New York, New York 10028